Measuring Thinking Skills in the Classroom

Revised Edition

Richard J. Stiggins

Evelyn Rubel

Edys Quellmalz

Northwest Regional Educational Laboratory

*Produced in cooperation
with the NEA Mastery in Learning Project*

nea PROFESSIONAL LIBRARY

National Education Association
Washington, D.C.

The Authors

Richard J. Stiggins is Director, Center for Performance Assessment, Northwest Regional Educational Laboratory, Portland, Oregon.

Evelyn Rubel is a fourth grade teacher, Liberty Elementary School, Salem, Oregon.

Edys Quellmalz, an assessment and curriculum design consultant in the development of thinking and writing skills, has served on the graduate faculty of Stanford University and the Center for the Study of Evaluation, University of California at Los Angeles.

The Advisory Panel

Loree Bunch, Special Education teacher, Conejo Elementary School, Thousand Oaks, California

Loretta Guthrie, first grade teacher, Westwood School, Dalton, Georgia

James Kelly, eighth grade Social Studies teacher, Richard Butler School, Butler, New Jersey

Doug Tuthill, Philosophy and Psychology teacher, St. Petersburg High School, Florida

Jerry Wilkening, sixth grade teacher, Mount Vernon Community Center School, Alexandria, Virginia

Note

This publication was developed under Contract No. 400-83-0005 with the National Institute of Education, U.S. Department of Education. Opinions expressed in this publication do not necessarily reflect the position of the National Institute of Education and no official endorsement should be inferred.

Library of Congress Cataloging-in-Publication Data

Stiggins, Richard J.
   Measuring thinking skills in the classroom.

"Produced in cooperation with the NEA Mastery in Learning Project."
   Bibliography: p.
   1. Critical thinking—United States—Ability
testing.   2. Students—United States—Rating of.
   3. Examinations—United States—Design and
construction.   Rubel, Evelyn.   II. Quellmalz,
Edys.   III. Title.
   LB1590.3.S78   1988   370.15'2   88–1530
   ISBN 0-8106-0211-3

Contents

Chapter 1
Measuring Thinking Skills

There are one-story intellects, two-story intellects and three-story intellects with skylights. All fact collectors who have no aim beyond their facts are one-story people. Two-story people compare, reason, generalize, using the labor of the fact collectors as their own. Three-story people idealize, imagine, predict—their best illumination comes from above through the skylight.
—Oliver Wendell Holmes

If we teachers are going to teach critical thinking skills, we must plan and conduct our instruction in a careful manner. We must be able to determine which thinking skills students have already mastered and which they have yet to learn. In addition, we must be able to measure the impact of our instruction. In order to diagnose students' difficulties and monitor and evaluate their learning, we must be capable of measuring thinking skills in the classroom on a day-to-day basis. Measuring student achievement is a challenge, even when our goal is simply to measure recall of information. When we add the challenge of measuring students' ability to use that information to think critically and solve problems, the measurement process becomes increasingly complex.

In the past, we have failed to meet the challenge of evaluating thinking skills. A recent study of tests developed by teachers in a large metropolitan school district reveals that nearly three-quarters of the thousands of test items analyzed across grade levels tested recall of information (2).* Very few items tested students' ability to apply higher-order thinking skills. Few tested their ability to analyze available knowledge or to draw inferences about or with newly learned information. Few tested their ability to draw conclusions and to support evaluative judgments.

Yet, the development of thinking skills is becoming a higher and higher priority among educators and critics of education. As this interest has intensified, the inadequacy of our current instruction in and our assessment of these skills has become apparent. Edys Quellmalz has characterized the problem as follows:

> The call for attention to higher-order thinking skills rings throughout the educational system. Educators, policymakers and the public agree that higher-order skills are important but neglected in curricula and tests and, therefore, underdeveloped in students. We have sufficient rhetoric and evidence to establish the need for renewed emphasis on higher-order skills; what we lack is consensus on what higher-order thinking is, on how to measure its outcomes, and on how to teach it. Furthermore, despite the lip service paid to the significance of higher-order thinking skills, administrators, teachers and students may view thinking skills as tangential to required courses of study, as appropriate only for older, high achieving students, or as too demanding of time and effort. To compound the problem, administrative and economic support for projects have often been too weak or short-lived to establish and maintain thinking skills assessment and curricula. (5, p. 1)

---

*Numbers in parentheses appearing in the text refer to the References on page 27.

4

Efforts are now under way on several fronts to begin to deal with this problem. For instance, researchers are striving to understand the thinking process and translate their understanding into practical classroom terms (4). Authors of instructional materials are writing texts and study guides that go beyond recall [see, for example, *Exploring Our World*, a junior high social studies text by W. Joyce and others (3)]. Several states, including California, Connecticut, and Colorado, are instituting state-wide assessments of critical thinking skills with the intent of raising the teaching of these skills to a higher level of priority in local curricula. Many other states are launching new instructional programs in this area.

We have designed this guide to contribute to the growing effort to teach critical thinking skills by providing teachers with simple but very powerful tools to use in measuring those skills on a day-to-day basis in the classroom. Specifically, it provides—

- a simple, usable set of definitions of thinking skills,

- brief explanations of three common forms of classroom assessment, and

- a planning strategy for crossing levels of thinking skills with forms of classroom assessment in such a way as to use assessment to promote student skill in higher-level cognitive operations.

In addition, we offer a series of very practical guidelines for making assessment planning strategies work effectively in the classroom.

We have written this guide for teachers. However, those who support teachers' instructional efforts (administrators, curriculum specialists, etc.) will also find it useful. The strategies we discuss can be applied to all subjects at all grade levels. For purposes of illustration, we have included a range of assessment examples covering concepts taught in science, social studies, and language arts (composition and literature), and pertaining to elementary, junior high, and high school levels of instruction. To aid the reader in learning and using these strategies, we have provided space throughout the guide for users to fill in examples relevant to their particular context. This feature makes it easy for teachers and others to begin to address issues related to teaching critical thinking skills.

THE BENEFITS OF ASSESSING

Teachers who know how to assess thinking skills derive many benefits, the most important of which we have already mentioned. As educators, we want students to do far more than just restate facts we have taught them. Our goal is to teach students *to use* the information at their disposal. We want them to think. Very simply, we are doomed to fall far short of this goal if we are unable to monitor development and measure student mastery of the thinking skills we seek to impart. If we cannot measure the extent to which a skill has been mastered, we cannot determine what to teach next. If we cannot measure the skills we teach, we cannot know if instruction is effective.

From another perspective, it is important for teachers to be able to measure higher-order thinking skills because their tests do more to tell students what is expected of them than does any other single factor. Much of what students study and learn is dependent on what they think educators expect of them—and they develop those expectations based on tests. If teachers test recall, students learn the facts; if teachers test more, students prepare themselves to deliver more.

From still another perspective, teachers who know how to devise their own measures of thinking skills have more freedom in designing instructional plans. They can adjust their questions to new textbooks and not be chained to text materials that don't teach thinking skills. Teachers who are adept at measuring thinking skills can tailor their instruction and assessments to the unique needs and capabilities of their students, thus individualizing instruction cognitively. And they can critique text materials being considered for adoption with regard to the possible influence on students' thinking skills.

This role of the teacher as a critical consumer also becomes important in another context. Teachers who are skilled at measuring thinking skills can review and evaluate standardized tests being considered for adoption by their district—thus ensuring that the tests selected match the instructional priorities in their classrooms. Teachers must select published tests that not only cover appropriate content—i.e., match the objectives of the teachers whose students are to be tested—but also measure thinking skills taught in the classroom. To the extent that a test fails to match local content or thinking skill priorities, that test will provide invalid information regarding student achievement.

THE ASSESSMENT PLANNING FRAMEWORK

Our goal is to explain how basic thinking skills—skills students must use in solving significant academic and life problems—can be measured using three common forms of classroom assessment. To achieve this goal, we will provide instruction in how to measure the five fundamental cognitive operations—recall, analysis, comparison, inference, and evaluation—using oral questioning during instruction, objective paper-and-pencil test items, and performance assessment based on teacher observation and subjective judgment. These elements are defined in detail below. When combined, they provide a simple, yet comprehensive framework for measuring thinking skills.

In preparing a guide to address this framework, we have made several assumptions about the teachers who will use the guide. We assumed that teachers are (a) proficient at writing basic test items using common formats (e.g., essay, multiple-choice, true/false), (b) proficient at designing and using measures of student achievement based on observation and professional judgment, and (c) knowledgeable about the subject matter they teach. We have made these assumptions for two reasons. First, space limitations do not allow instruction in these areas. And second, these skills are not essential to *understanding* our planning strategies. However, if teachers are to use these planning strategies effectively in the classroom, it is very important that they have basic test development skills and a thorough knowledge of content. For the reader who wants assistance in these areas, we suggest the resources listed in Appendix A.

DEFINING THINKING SKILLS

If we are to measure thinking skills effectively and efficiently in the demanding, fact-paced world of the classroom, we must start with clear and usable definitions. The task of specifying the domain of thinking skills has challenged philosophers, cognitive psychologists, and subject-matter experts for decades—even centuries. Rather than detailing that history of discovery, we have synthesized prior conceptual frameworks into one that we think will suffice for most classrooms (5). When we compare the lists of basic cognitive operations involved in the problem-solving and critical thinking skills that have been proposed by philosophers, psychologists, and educators, five fundamental components recur: recall, analysis, comparison, inference, and evaluation. These skills are defined in Table 1. They are used at varying points in the problem-solving and critical thinking processes as students (1) identify the problem type or central issue, (2) find and identify relevant information, (3) connect relevant information, and (4) evaluate solutions and conclusions. These skills are also major forms of explanations and inquiry in their own rights.

We do not characterize these skills as a rigid hierachy because there may be a wide range of difficulty within each category. Analysis can be simple or complex, depending upon the scope and the complexity of the problem; similarly, evaluation can be easy or difficult. Generally speaking, evaluation and inference draw upon the other reasoning operations as well. The primary distinction among these five categories of thinking skills lies in the different ways in which students relate and use information.

Here are some simple illustrations of how the higher-order reasoning skills appear as major forms of explanations and inquiry in three general subject-matter areas:

	Science	Social Science	Literature
Analyze	Identify components of a process, features of animate and inanimate objects	Analyze components of arguments, elements of an event	Identify components of literary, expository, and persuasive discourse
Compare	Compare properties of objects, components of processes	Compare causes and/or effects of separate events; social, political, economic, geographic features	Compare meanings, themes, plots, characters, settings, arguments
Infer	Draw conclusions; make predictions; pose hypothesis tests and explanations	Predict, hypothesize, conclude, interpret using historical, social, political, economic, geographic information	Infer theme, significance, characters' motivations; interrelationships of literary elements
Evaluate	Evaluate soundness of procedures, credibility of conclusions, significance of findings	Evaluate credibility of arguments, decisions, reports; significance	Evaluate believability, significance, form, completeness, clarity

Others have subdivided thinking skills differently. Benjamin Bloom and others (1) have suggested six levels of cognitive operation that have been extensively studied and applied by educators. These operations, outlined in Appendix C, might well have been substituted for our five levels in this guide. We have adopted those described above to illustrate our assessment planning strategy because of their simplicity. But the key to success in measuring and teaching thinking skills is to adopt a taxonomy of skills and use it consistently.

Table 1
SUMMARY OF THINKING SKILLS

Level	Definition	Relation to Bloom Taxonomy
Recall	Most tasks require that students recognize or remember key facts, definitions, concepts, rules, and principles. Recall questions require students to repeat verbatim or to paraphrase given information. To recall information, students need most often to rehearse or practice it, and then to associate it with other, related concepts. The Bloom taxonomy levels of knowledge and comprehension are subsumed here, since verbatim repetition and translation into the student's own words represent acceptable evidence of learning and understanding.	Recall Comprehension
Analysis	In this operation, students divide a whole into component elements. Generally the part/whole relationships and the cause/effect relationships that characterize knowledge within subject domains are essential components of more complex tasks. The components can be the distinctive characteristics of objects or ideas, or the basic actions of procedures or events. This definition of analysis is the same as that in the Bloom taxonomy.	Analysis
Comparison	These tasks require students to recognize or explain similarities and differences. Simple comparisons require attention to one or a few very obvious attributes or component processes, while complex comparisons require identification of and differentiation among many attributes or component actions. This category relates to some of the skills in the Bloom level of analysis. The separate comparison category emphasizes the distinct information processing required when students go beyond breaking the whole into parts in order to compare similarities and differences.	Analysis
Inference	Both deductive and inductive reasoning fall in this category. In deductive tasks, students are given a generalization and are required to recognize or explain the evidence that relates to it. Applications of rules and "if–then" relationships require inference. In inductive tasks, students are given the evidence or details and are required to come up with the generalization. Hypothesizing, predicting, concluding, and synthesizing all require students to relate and integrate information. Inductive and deductive reasoning relate to the Bloom levels of application and synthesis. Application of a rule is one kind of deductive reasoning; synthesis, putting parts together to form a generalization, occurs in both inductive and deductive reasoning.	Application Synthesis
Evaluation	These tasks require students to judge quality, credibility, worth, or practicality. Generally we expect students to use established criteria and explain how these criteria are or are not met. The criteria might be established rules of evidence, logic, or shared values. Bloom's levels of synthesis and evaluation are involved in this category. To evaluate, students must assemble and explain the interrelationship of evidence and reasons in support of their conclusion (synthesis). Explanation of criteria for reaching a conclusion is unique to evaluative reasoning.	Synthesis Evaluation

FORMS OF CLASSROOM ASSESSMENT

The measurement of student achievement can take many forms in the classroom: some formal and some informal; some individual and some group; some standardized for all classrooms and some tailored to the specific classroom context. For the purpose of illustrating these measurement strategies, we have selected three of the most common forms of assessment: oral questions asked during instruction, paper-and-pencil tests, and performance tests. Each is described below.

Oral Questions

These are the questions teachers ask during instruction to (1) stimulate thought and discussion among students and (2) gather a brief sample of evidence by which to monitor students' skill development and achievement. Oral questions can stimulate students to think creatively, stretching and exploring interpretations of the knowledge at their disposal. They can be directed to an individual student (volunteer or not) or asked of the class as a whole to stimulate a discussion. They are open-ended, often allowing for more than one correct answer. For example, the teacher might ask, "What are some ways we might have avoided using the atomic bomb at the end of World War II?" Questions might be asked at a rapid-fire pace, demanding brief responses and quick follow-up questioning by the teacher, or they might be posed in a more thoughtful manner, allowing extended explanation and interpretation.

This is an informal mode of monitoring and assessment that is most often an integral part of instruction. Although it is not part of the formal testing for grading purposes, oral questioning is very much a part of the classroom monitoring and evaluation environment. For more detailed suggestions in this area, see Wilen (8).

Paper-and-Pencil Tests

This form of assessment includes the test items teachers prepare for their more formal written tests and quizzes that are used for diagnosis, grading, or placement. Such test questions have traditionally been used to measure students' ability to think convergently to arrive at a best or correct answer; however, open-ended formats are also used. The student responds in some written form using words and/or symbols. Formats include selection items (multiple-choice, true/false, matching), supply items (fill-in, short answer), and essay items (limited and extended response). Paper-and-pencil tests can be used for in-progress monitoring or for more formal assessment conducted after instruction is completed. Many educators tend to link selection items with the measurement of recall and essay items with the measurement of higher-order thinking skills. However, as we proceed through this guide, we will show that multiple-choice and true/false items can also serve to measure some higher-order thinking skills. For example:

> Was infantry invasion of Japan a viable alternative to the use of the atomic bomb to end World War II? If so, why? If not, why not?
>
> a. Yes; transport ships were available in sufficient numbers.
>
> b. Yes; island defenses in Japan were minimal.
>
> c. No; estimated casualties would have been much greater.
>
> d. No; Japan was on the verge of having an atomic bomb.

Performance Tests

With this form of assessment, the teacher observes and judges an activity in progress or a product developed by the student. Students are presented with a set of instructions (the performance exercise), they respond in some overtly behavioral manner, and the teacher observes and evaluates the quality of the behavior and/or the resulting product in terms of prespecified performance standards or criteria (7). Performance tests might be formal assessments used for grading purposes or less formal assessments integrated into instruction. Such assessments play key roles in the measurement of reasoning strategies, communication skills, motor development, foreign language proficiency, science laboratory procedures, and other skills. Performance assessments call upon students to demonstrate what they know by doing it and, in some instances, to explain their strategies.

These three forms of assessment are included in this guide because many teachers already design and use them. Therefore, teachers can control the extent to which their assessments measure more than simple recall. Tests that accompany textbooks and standardized achievement tests also measure student achievement, but teachers typically have less control over these. To the extent that teachers can play a role in the selection of texts or published tests and want those materials to measure specific higher-order thinking skills, they can use information presented in this guide to select materials that reflect higher-order objectives of instruction in their classrooms.

THE BASIC ASSESSMENT PLANNING CHART

By combining the five types of thinking and the three forms of classroom assessment described above, we create a framework or chart to guide classroom measurement of key concepts.

ASSESSMENT PLANNING CHART

	Oral Questioning	Paper-and- Pencil Tests	Performance Assessment
Recall			
Analysis			
Comparison			
Inference			
Evaluation			

Using this chart, we can select one element of instruction at a particular grade level—say, an elementary science unit on the Solar System—and show how the nature of the assessment varies across levels and forms of assessment.

Beginning with simple *recall*, during instruction we might pose this question to the class:

Today, we are beginning a unit on the Solar System. What is the Solar System?

Or we might pose an *analysis* question:

Let's see if we can identify the parts of our Solar System.

10

Oral questioning in class might also deal with *comparisons*:

> We have been sending unmanned space flights to Mars. How is Mars like Earth? How is it different? What about size, distance from the Sun, surface, atmosphere?

The completed chart on page 12 illustrates the remaining categories under oral questioning.

Moving to more formal paper-and-pencil testing, the questions might look like this:

Recall: Define *solar system*.

Analysis: Match each planet with its unique characteristics:

_____ Earth	a. Has rings of gas and ice crystals
_____ Mars	b. Appears red in night sky
_____ Venus	c. Is farthest from the Sun
_____ Saturn	d. Is known to support life
_____ Pluto	e. Is called the evening star
	f. Revolves around the Sun
	g. Is part of the Milky Way.

The remaining paper-and-pencil testing for other skill categories also appears on the chart on page 12.

Finally, performance assessment (observation and judgment) can serve as an instructional function:

> Choose the name of a planet. I (the teacher) am the Sun. Put yourself in orbit around me considering where you are in relation to other planets and how far you are from the Sun. Use one inch to represent each million miles of distance.

For each individual child, this measures recall (remembering order and distance), analysis and comparison (reflecting relationships among planets), and inference (using a measurement scale). For those students who place themselves incorrectly, the teacher can ask follow-up oral questions to determine which component skills have not been mastered.

In the next chapter, we provide examples of assessment charts covering concepts studied in a number of subjects at various grade levels. We follow these examples with specific and very practical guidelines for developing and using such charts for your own classroom assessment.

ASSESSMENT PLANNING CHART

GRADE LEVEL _____ Elementary _____ SUBJECT _____ Science _____ TOPIC _____ Solar System

	ORAL	TEST	PERFORMANCE
RECALL	Today we begin a unit on the Solar System. What do you think the Solar System is?	Define *solar system*.	Choose the name of a planet. I (the teacher) am the Sun. Put yourself in orbit around me considering where you are in relation to other planets and how far you are from the Sun. Use one inch to represent each million miles of distance. (Note: A large space will be needed even with this small scale.) Performance criteria: Recall: Do students remember order and distance? Comparison: Can they reflect relationships among planets? Inference: Can they use the distance scale?
ANALYSIS	Let's see if we can think of all of the parts of our Solar System.	Which of the following is NOT a part of our solar system? a. the sun b the moon c. Mars d. the constellation Orion	
COMPARISON	We've been sending unmanned space flights to Mars. How is Mars like Earth? How is it different?	The Sun and the planets are all components in our Solar System. How does the Sun differ from the planets?	
INFERENCE	The planets rotate around the Sun and revolve in a definite pattern. What do you think might happen if one of the planets suddenly changed orbit?	Imagine that we discovered a new planet. Which of the following are we likely to know *first*? a. Its size b. How many moons it has c. Surface terrain.	
EVALUATION	Which part of the Solar System is most important to us here on Earth? Why?	If you were selected to travel to Mars, would you go? Why or why not?	

Chapter 2

Learning to Plan the Assessment

Questions are the creative acts of intelligence.

—Frank Kingdom

This chapter provides examples of completed and partially completed Assessment Planning Charts. Each chart focuses on one topic or concept and presents examples of how this concept can be assessed for all five skill categories using all three forms of assessment. To illustrate, we have selected topics that are somewhat familiar to all from three general subject-matter areas at three instructional levels:

- Elementary English: Poetry (page 14)
- Junior High Social Studies: Electoral College (page 15)
- Junior High Science: Energy (page 16)
- High School Social Studies: Branches of Government (page 17)

STUDY STEP 1: REVIEWING THE MODEL CHARTS

As a study strategy, we recommend that you proceed through these charts one by one, examining the exercises presented in each. Occasionally, we have left a cell blank in the chart. You are invited to fill in the blanks. Try to complete each chart as well as you can. If some cells are just too difficult to fill in, *leave them blank*. You can return and complete them later.

STUDY STEP 2: USING THE GENERIC CHART (page 18)

Now that you have completed this review and fill-in task, it may have become apparent that questions tapping the same level of cognitive operation have a great deal in common across charts, even though the topic changes. This fact has allowed us to develop a generic chart—a kind of formula chart in which we have provided generic questions and the teacher simply fills in the concept or topic to be assessed.

After you have attempted to complete all of the charts in Study Step 1, study the generic chart and use its formula questions to fill in any blanks you were unable to complete the first time.

STUDY STEP 3: USING THE FORMULA TO GENERATE A COMPLETE CHART

The next step in the learning process is to use the generic chart to complete an entire chart on a topic of interest and at a level appropriate to you. Here we must add a caution. We do not recommend ongoing reliance on the generic chart. It is included here merely as a learning aid. Once you understand the levels and the process of creating an Assessment Planning Chart, you will realize that many different kinds of probes can trigger student thinking. We illustrate this fact later. But for now, use the generic chart to generate a complete Assessment Planning Chart on a topic of relevance to you. If you need to make minor revisions to the wording of the generic item form to write a good excise, feel free to do so. It is intended for flexible use.

ASSESSMENT PLANNING CHART

GRADE LEVEL _____ Elementary   SUBJECT _____ English   TOPIC _____ Poetry

	ORAL	TEST	PERFORMANCE
RECALL	Let's see if we can tell what poetry is.	A haiku has _____ lines and _____ syllables.	Compare some work of local poets. Choose the one you like best. As you know, artists are often not ''recognized'' until after their deaths so they often live in poverty. You serve on a board which could help this poet you have chosen. How would you go about convincing the board to give funds to this particular poet? Prepare your materials for convincing. Try them out on the class.
ANALYSIS	Let's see how many different kinds of poetry we can list.	Tell the purpose of an acrostic in poetry and write a brief example.	
COMPARISON	Let's compare several kinds of poetry as to rhyming technique, rhythm, structure, etc. Shall we first compare a limerick and a couplet?	Put an H if a haiku, a C if a couplet, and a D if a diamente. ____ a. Has 17 syllables ____ c. Has 7 lines ____ b. Has 2 lines ____ d. Has 3 lines.	
INFERENCE	Have several poems ready for use on the overhead, written on the board, or prepared as handouts. Students choose a poem and imagine how it might sound written as another form. Put examples on the board.	Rewrite this haiku as a limerick.	
EVALUATION	Do you think it's important to encourage the writing of poetry? Why or why not?	Some poetry is very structured. Do you prefer it to the less structured? Why or why not? Cite two examples of the kind of poetry you prefer.	

ASSESSMENT PLANNING CHART

GRADE LEVEL ___ Junior High ___ SUBJECT ___ Social Studies ___ TOPIC ___ Electoral College

	ORAL	TEST	PERFORMANCE
RECALL	What is the electoral college?	As a member of the electoral college, you must vote: a. According to your own judgment b. As your constituency voted c. As the party tells you d. Only if you wish to do so.	Assume you're a U.S. senator. Propose a constitutional amendment that would make the popular vote the sole criterion for electing a president. Your amendment would do away with the electoral college. Prepare a speech to Congress defending your amendment. Be sure to— a. Analyze all elements of the issue, b. Compare elections with and without the college, c. Show how the voters are likely to react, and d. State and defend your values. (Or conduct a simulated debate on the Senate floor.)
ANALYSIS	How does the electoral college work?	Analyze the steps in the presidential election process, showing where the electoral college comes into play.	
COMPARISON	How do the social conditions that existed when the electoral college was formed differ from conditions now?	What is meant by the election theme "one person, one vote," and how does that relate to the electoral college?	
INFERENCE	If you were a presidential candidate elected by popular vote, could you still lose the election? How?	In which state is the electorate likely to oppose the use of the electoral college: a. California b. Illinois c. Etc.	
EVALUATION	Should the electoral college be abolished? Why or why not?	Which of the following is the best reason for maintaining the electoral college? a. Tradition. b. Fairness to large states. c. Etc.	

ASSESSMENT PLANNING CHART

GRADE LEVEL ———— Junior High SUBJECT ———— Science TOPIC ———— Energy

	ORAL	TEST	PERFORMANCE
RECALL	Today we're beginning a unit on energy. Let's develop a definition for the word energy.		You are planning to build a new house. Compare the energy sources. Decide which you'll use in your house. Explain how you'll use the sources you've chosen. Also tell why you chose that source for that particular job. You may draw the plans showing the various places of energy use if you wish. If you do this with a good explanation key, then you need not write an explanation.
ANALYSIS		What are the three effects of mining and burning coal?	
COMPARISON	Let's compare the costs of using the following energy sources: nuclear, solar, coal, water, wood, and wind.		
INFERENCE	If we were suddenly cut off from the supply of petroleum from the Middle East, what would be some short-term problems? What would be some long-term solutions to those problems?		
EVALUATION		Write a short paper telling which energy source is the most important for the United States. Give at least three reasons why it's the most important.	

ASSESSMENT PLANNING CHART

GRADE LEVEL ___ High School ___ SUBJECT ___ Social Studies ___ TOPIC ___ Branches of Government ___

	ORAL	TEST	PERFORMANCE
RECALL	Who's in charge of the executive branch of government? The judicial branch? The legislature?		Set the class up as a democracy with three branches of government. Go through the actual process of passing a law. Determine if students know and can carry out each function. Strive to demonstrate the interactions among branches.
ANALYSIS		What can the executive branch do about an unfair law?	
COMPARISON	In America we have Congress. In Canada their legislature is called Parliament. How do they differ in structure? *OR* Compare the structure of the federal government with that of your state government.		
INFERENCE		You've decided motorcycles cause too many accidents. You'd like them banned from federally funded highways. To which government branch would you first appeal? a. Executive b. Judicial c. Legislative	
EVALUATION	Which branch of the government is the most important? Why?		

ASSESSMENT PLANNING CHART

GRADE LEVEL _____   SUBJECT _____   Generic Chart   TOPIC _____

	ORAL	TEST	PERFORMANCE
RECALL	What is _____?	What is the best definition for the term _____? a. b. c.	Give a speech/plan a debate in which you use what you know about _____ to judge its _____. Give reasons to support your point of view.
ANALYSIS	How does _____ work?	What are the basic elements (ingredients) of _____?	
COMPARISON	Compare the _____ to _____.	What is the major difference between _____ and _____?	
INFERENCE	What do you think would happen if _____?	Which of the following is a likely result of _____? a. b. c.	
EVALUATION	In your opinion, which of the following is the best solution to the problem of _____? (List options.) Why is this best?	Here is the issue: _____ Which side are you on and why?	

STUDY STEP 4: ADDING VARIETY TO THE QUESTIONS

Now let's move from the formula chart to the generation of charts with a greater variety of questions.

The first key to expanding the range of questions you can pose is to focus on the trigger or action verb used to describe the problem to the students. Start with these and add some of your own if you can:

If you want to measure:	Use these key words in the exercise:		Illustration
Recall	define identify label list name	repeat what when who	List the names of the main characters in the story.
Analysis	subdivide break down separate	categorize sort	Break the story down into different parts.
Comparison	compare contrast	differentiate distinguish	Compare the themes of these two stories.
Inference	deduce predict infer speculate	anticipate what if . . . apply conclude	How might we make this character more believable?
Evaluation	evaluate judge assess appraise defend	argue recommend debate why critique	Evaluate this story. Is it well written? Why or why not?

The second key to expanding the range of questions you can pose is to plug these action words into a growing list of generic questions. Again, consider these and add some of your own if you can:

Recall

- Define the word _____.
- What is a _____?
- Label the following _____.
- Identify the _____ in this _____.
- Who did _____?

Analysis

- What are the basic elements (ingredients) in a _____?
- What is/are the function(s) of _____?
- Inventory the parts of _____.
- Categorize the _____ of _____.
- Sort the _____.
- Analyze the following _____.

Comparison

- Compare the _____ before and after.
- Contrast the _____ to the _____.
- Differentiate between _____ and _____.

Inference

- Hypothesize what will happen if _____.
- Predict what would be true if _____.
- Conclude what the result will be if _____.
- What if _____ had happened instead?
- What does this information suggest?
- Given this situation (problem), what should you do?
- What rule applies in this case?

Evaluation

- What do you believe about _____?
- Judge what would be the best way to solve the problem of _____. Why did you decide that?
- Evaluate whether you would _____ or _____ in this situation. Why?
- Decide if _____ was worth it. Explain.

Use these lists of action verbs and questions to generate a complete chart on another topic of relevance to you. Use the chart on page 22 to do this.

FINAL STEP: A PROGRESS CHECK

In the space provided next to each exercise, enter the letter that represents the thinking skill category reflected in the item (see Appendix B for the answers):

R=Recall   A=Analysis   C=Comparison   I=Inference   E=Evaluation

_____   1. What are three functions of the liver?

_____   2. Let's brainstorm what would happen if the sun did not come up tomorrow.

_____   3. Define the word *mitasis*.

_____   4. Which of the following menus is the best? Why?

20

_____ 5. Which menu provides more complete protein?

_____ 6. Should the use of computers be abolished in the classroom? Why or why not?

_____ 7. Who is the author of *Where the Sidewalk Ends*?

_____ 8. If we mix these chemicals together, what do you suppose will happen?

_____ 9. Look at the chart showing the number of meals Americans have eaten away from home over the last three years. How have eating habits changed?

_____ 10. What are three purposes of an unmanned space flight to Jupiter?

_____ 11. What are the functions of our eyelashes?

_____ 12. Which do you think will have greater impact on your life, the invention of the computer or our ability to travel in space? Why?

_____ 13. If you were going outside and it was snowing quite hard, which of the following would you need from your closet?

_____ a. Your umbrella

_____ b. Your lightweight jacket

_____ c. Your warm boots

_____ d. Your sandals.

_____ 14. You hate rain, but know it is necessary. What are three purposes it serves?

_____ 15. In the Northwest it rains and snows a lot. Which is more vital to create the supply of water necessary for summer use?

_____ 16. What are some jobs a migrant worker might perform in getting a crop of lettuce to market?

_____ 17. Haiku is a form of _____.

_____ 18. Look at these three paintings. Which makes the most use of vivid colors?

_____ 19. Suppose we had not dropped the bombs on Hiroshima and Nagasaki. How else might we have defeated the Japanese?

_____ 20. Which is a better snack for you, a fresh peach or a dish of frozen peach yogurt? Why?

THE KEY TO SUCCESSFUL ASSESSMENT

Any of the 20 exercises listed above could measure the recall of facts and information, if prior instruction has caused students to memorize the answers. When this occurs, regardless of the appearance of the item, it does *not* measure higher-order thinking skills. The key to successful assessment of thinking skills is to pose novel problems for which students have not memorized answers. Such problems require that students think.

ASSESSMENT PLANNING CHART

GRADE LEVEL _____ ORAL

SUBJECT _____ TEST

TOPIC _____ PERFORMANCE

	ORAL	TEST	PERFORMANCE
RECALL			
ANALYSIS			
COMPARISON			
INFERENCE			
EVALUATION			

Chapter 3

Making Assessment Work in the Classroom

The easily observable fact is that children are passionately eager to make as much sense as they can of the world around them, are extremely good at it, and do it as scientists do, by creating knowledge out of experience. Children observe, wonder, find, or make, and then test the answers to the questions they ask themselves. When they are not actually prevented from doing these things, they continue to do them and to get better and better at it.

—John Holt

Now that the basic structure and elements of the Assessment Planning Chart are in place, how do we make it work for us in the classroom? Here are some simple guidelines.

DEVELOPING QUESTIONS FOR DAILY USE IN THE CLASSROOM

1. To repeat an earlier point, learn and use a set of categories such as the one presented here. Ours works well for us, but it may not meet your needs. Many teachers are familiar with the taxonomy of educational objectives in the cognitive domain developed by Bloom and others (1). For those who prefer that framework, the categories of the cognitive domain are defined and illustrated with key action verbs in Appendix C. But the key point is to choose one, learn it, and refer to it for *consistency*.
2. Use textbooks as a guide in selecting priority topics to be assessed throughout the range of thinking skill categories. This will assure a match between what content is taught and what is tested.
3. Actually develop written charts for key units and crucial concepts *before* teaching them. This will save planning and test development time, and it will give you a written record to use every time you teach that unit over the years.
4. Set up a file or notebook of completed charts. This will save time later when you want to retrieve them.
5. Carefully evaluate the assessments that often accompany textbooks. Even though they come from the textbook publisher, they may not match the cognitive categories covered in the text or covered in your instruction in class. If they don't match, either adapt and improve them, or use your own assessments.
6. Develop questions that encourage creative thought. This provides students elbow room—opportunities for answers that might not be quite so common or usual. Divergent thought develops the following, which are the basis for creative thinking:

   ● Flexibility of ideas
   ● Fluency of ideas
   ● Spontaneity
   ● Uniqueness.

23

7. Teach your students the different categories of thinking skills. Then they'll know your expectations. Post the categories and key trigger words prominently in the classroom so you and your students can refer to them during discussion.

8. Involve students in the process of brainstorming questions at different levels for their own tests. One person's thought may trigger something in another's mind. A new question is developed. This concept, called *hitchhiking*, will help students internalize the levels, and it will save you test development time.

9. Get together with other teachers who are using the same text or teaching the same unit to brainstorm questions.

10. Ask students what they would like to know about a new, upcoming subject. Then they will have something at stake in the development of the unit and will better understand its purpose.

MANAGING THE ASSESSMENT PROCESS

1. When you ask a question, wait for a response. Teachers, on the average, wait less than a second after asking a question. Yet according to M.B. Rowe (6), a three- to five-second wait time seems to improve both student responses and teacher reactions. What happens to students when teachers wait longer for them to answer? Rowe suggests that—

   - The length of student responses increases. Explanatory statements increase in length.
   - The number of unsolicited, but appropriate responses increases.
   - Failure to respond decreases.
   - The confidence of students increases.
   - The incidence of speculative, creative thinking increases.
   - Teacher-centered teaching decreases, and student-centered interaction increases.
   - Students give more evidence before and after inference statements.
   - The number of questions asked by students increases.
   - The number of activities proposed by students increases.
   - Slow students contribute more.
   - The variety of types of responses increases. There is more reacting to each other, structuring of procedures, and soliciting.
   - Discipline problems decrease.

   Teachers change also:

   - They exhibit more flexible types of responses.
   - The number and kinds of questions they ask change.
   - Their expectations regarding student performance are modified. They become less likely to expect only the brighter students to reply, and they view their classes as having fewer academically slower students.

2. Set up questions on 3 × 5 cards. These come in five colors and white so each level of question can be on a different color card.

   - You can use these when it is time to prepare your written assessment.
   - If you are using the inquiry method, you can put these cards in a file box for classroom use. Students can choose which card they would like to work on individually or with a group.

3. Avoid questions that can be answered with a "yes" or a "no." If you do use them, call for an explanation of the response from the student.

4. When a student has incompletely or incorrectly answered a question, give some sustaining feedback; follow up with a question such as—

   - Can you explain that further?
   - Why did you think that?
   - Did you consider _____?
   - Did you remember to _____?
   - On what information do you base that?
   - What evidence suggests that?
   - Is there another way of looking at this?

   This helps the student arrive at a defensible answer and develops higher-order thinking skills.

5. Whenever possible during oral questioning, use all the component categories from lower to higher order to advantage. Begin with recall and proceed step by step to evaluation, making all the stops along the way. In this way, you can bring students along. Or if you start at a higher level and a student has difficulty, go back to recall and work back up to the level where the error occurred. This will reveal the nature of the error made.

6. Ask one student to paraphrase or explain what another has said.

   - John, could you say what Mary just said in different words?
   - In other words, what was Sam saying, Pete?

7. Keep the whole class involved.

   - Call on nonvolunteers regularly so those who are not raising hands must remain tuned in.
   - Have them listening in order to add to what someone else has said. Have students frequently comment on or add to other answers.
   - Have students raise their hands, click their fingers, etc., if they agree.
   - Have students who are preparing to write a report comment on or evaluate the discussion.

8. Frequently have students consider questions in small groups.

   - This offers emotional support and a feeling of inclusion.
   - Usually students will be less anxious.
   - This allows students to pool information and generally results in the development of more ideas.
   - Individual talents can be shared and/or developed.

9. Use questions for written as well as oral work. Several groups can work with the same question. While five groups are discussing and working on the question for a written or oral report, you can be talking with and questioning another group.

10. If students are working in groups, be sure they are aware of all sources for information. Develop with them a list of where they can go for information.

11. Be sure students who are working in groups know how to—

    - Organize their time;
    - Organize their paper, folders, files, etc.;
    - Listen actively; and
    - Discuss effectively.

12. Use your questions for other purposes.
   - Design a bulletin board full of questions.
   - Set up a learning center with lots of choices of things to do that require higher-order thinking skills.

13. Use your ability to develop questions to evaluate new textbooks and standardized tests that are being considered for use in your district.

14. Be sure students have learned (or know where to find) the knowledge upon which to develop higher-level thinking.

15. Be sure you have adequate knowledge of the subject area so you will be able to evaluate the thinking of your students.

16. Remember to use the various assessment categories for all work. Do not use higher-order skills during class discussions and then switch to recall for tests, or use higher-order skills for performance but stay at the recall level for daily assessment.

17. Encourage students to become the discussion leaders or moderators.

18. Encourage students to track their own development. They can—
   - Compare their progress to that of others or, perhaps, to their own during the previous year,
   - Rate themselves on rating scales reflecting levels,
   - Keep diaries or logs of evidence of effective functioning in all categories, and/or
   - Keep a file or folder of work produced and evaluations.

19. Have another teacher observe your class during a typical discussion and record the results. This simple chart might serve to keep track of the types of questions attempted—with correct responses circled:

Student	Recall	Analysis	Comparison	Inference	Evaluation
Jennifer	①I I①			①	
Scott				I I I	I①
Shaya		①I	I①	I①	
Travis	I	I			
Michael				I I	①I I①

When you keep such charts, it becomes easier at student or parent-teacher conference time to give some concrete information as to the thinking skills of a student.

20. Set criteria for grades that reflect the importance of moving beyond recall. Extra points might be given for higher-order skills—e.g., a recall question could be worth one point, whereas an evaluation question could be worth five.

Summary

As they continue to strive for educational improvement, educators are now focusing on the improvement of reasoning skills. These have become the new "basic skills." Many state departments of education and the prominent national associations of educators are launching major developmental efforts in this direction. One key to the success of these efforts will be each individual teacher's ability to measure thinking skills in a valid and reliable manner. This guide is designed to help teachers acquire the needed assessment skills.

We have defined workable categories of thinking skills, illustrated how these categories relate to three prominent modes of classroom assessment, and provided guidelines and practice in adapting assessments for actual classroom use. But this is only a start.

Two more components are critical to quality classroom assessment. (1) You must continue to practice with the Assessment Planning Chart. This will allow you to internalize the categories so they become second nature. You will be thinking in terms of thinking skills. (2) You must continue to learn the skills necessary for sound test item writing and performance assessment. Without these basic skills—and they don't take long to acquire—the foregoing cannot serve you well. Available resources are listed in Appendix A.

We suggest that you find a partner or form a small group to practice these skills. You will grow together as you learn much from each other.

References

1. Bloom, B. S., and others. *Taxonomy of Educational Objectives: Cognitive Domain*. New York: David McKay, 1956.

2. Fleming, M., and Chambers, B. "Teacher-Made Tests: Windows on the Classroom." In *Testing in the Schools*, edited by W. E. Hathaway. New Directions in Testing and Measurement, No. 19. San Francisco: Jossey-Bass, 1983.

3. Joyce, W., and others. *Exploring Our World: Latin America and Canada*. Chicago: Follett, 1980.

4. Quellmalz, E. S. "Developing Reasoning Skills." In *Teaching Thinking Skills: Theory and Practice*, edited by J. R. Baron and R. J. Sternberg. New York: Freeman, 1985.

5. _____. "Needed: Better Methods for Testing Higher-Order Thinking Skills." *Educational Leadership* 43, no. 2 (1985).

6. Rowe, M. B. "Specific Ways to Develop Better Communications." In *Creative Questioning and Sensitivity: Listening Techniques*, 2d ed., edited by R. Sund and A. Carin. Columbus, Ohio: Charles E. Merrill, 1978.

7. Stiggins, R. J. *Evaluating Students by Classroom Observation: Watching Students Grow*. Washington, D.C.: National Education Association, 1986.

8. Wilen, William W. *Questioning Skills, for Teachers*, 2d ed. Washington, D.C.: National Education Association, 1986.

Additional Resources for Classroom Assessment

Fleming, M., and Chambers, B. "Teacher-Made Tests: Windows on the Classroom." In *Testing in the Schools*, edited by W. E. Hathaway. New Directions in Testing and Measurement, No. 19. San Francisco: Jossey-Bass, 1983.

Using information gathered during a three-year analysis of teachers' tests in the Cleveland schools, Fleming and Chambers provide a unique and insightful glimpse of what teachers test, how they test, and (presumably) what they value in the curriculum. Initiated originally as a result of a court order to ensure that all district tests, including teacher-made tests, were administered, scored, and used in a nondiscriminatory manner, the district's test analysis probed test design, formatting, legibility, understandability, bias, and, most importantly, the nature and quality of the test items. Results showed that while the 342 tests from all grade levels and subject areas met requirements for nondiscriminatory use of questions, they displayed other surprising characteristics, particularly with respect to the types and levels of questions used most frequently.

After analyzing the kinds of questions used, Fleming and Chambers report that teachers overwhelmingly preferred short-answer questions and showed minimal interest in essay items. Less than 2 percent of the some 9,000 items reviewed were essay based. Teachers also relied heavily on test questions that sampled knowledge of facts. Knowledge of facts along with knowledge of terms and rules constituted almost 80 percent of the test questions reviewed. On the other hand, only a minimal number of test items required students to apply learning.

The results of this review, and of Fleming and Chambers's recognition that what we test is what students learn because tests inevitably shape the curriculum, prompted the development of a high-quality series of modules for in-service training on classroom testing. Titled *Four Keys to Better Classroom Testing* (see following reference), these teacher training materials recommend sound strategies for improving the design and quality of classroom tests.

Chambers, B. *Four Keys to Better Classroom Testing*. Princeton, N.J.: Educational Testing Service, 1984.

As a result of their evaluation of teacher-made tests, Fleming and Chambers (see previous reference), working in collaboration with ETS, have developed this in-service training package to help teachers improve the quality of their paper-and-pencil tests. The training materials provide teachers with detailed guidelines for overall test planning, test item construction (focusing on selection, supply, and essay items), test assembly, and test administration.

The package has three features that make it particularly worthwhile. First, the information presented is very practical. Second, while the material is of high technical quality, it is presented in a nontechnical manner. Assessment procedures are clearly explained and well illustrated. And third, major concepts are illustrated in several ways.

For the trainer who is not a testing specialist, the package includes a complete slide/tape presentation. For the user more conversant with testing concepts, transparencies are included to accompany the workshop presentations and exercises outlined in the trainer's manual. This training package is well worth the cost if the goal is to assist teachers in becoming better teachers.

Gronlund, N. E. *Constructing Achievement Tests*. Englewood Cliffs, N.J.: Prentice-Hall, 1982.

This relatively inexpensive paperback is among the most concise and practical introductory textbooks available on educational measurement. In a brief 140 pages, Gronlund distills the most important measurement guidelines for developing tests that accurately assess student achievement; standardized tests are not considered.

The author specifies and describes five steps for effective achievement testing: (1) specify the domain of skills to be measured, (2) develop a representative sample of assessment exercises, (3) assemble the exercises into an efficient form, (4) administer the assessment and carefully interpret its results, and (5) use these results to improve instruction.

Teachers interested in measuring higher-order thinking skills will find the author's thorough discussion of key issues in designing and planning a quality test helpful. Also included are simple, carefully illustrated guidelines for writing good test items; useful recommendations for designing and using essay tests; and a descriptive chapter on using performance-based measures in the classroom. Quality control guidelines for maximizing the reliability and validity of formal and informal classroom tests are also specifically covered.

In short, this instructional guide, written especially for teachers, is an excellent introduction to fundamental issues in educational measurement.

Spandel, V. *Classroom Applications of Writing Assessment: A Teacher's Handbook*. Portland, Oregon: Northwest Regional Educational Laboratory, 1981.

This handbook provides classroom teachers with (1) the basic principles for evaluating student wrting samples using holistic, analytical, and primary trait scoring; (2) extensive practice in applying these scoring strategies to hypothetical samples of student writing; and (3) a series of very practical and immediately useful ideas for using these scoring strategies in day-to-day writing instruction.

Writing assessment, notes Spandel, can be used in the classroom in many different ways. For example, some teachers have found that teaching students to evaluate one another's writing makes them better critics of their own work and, ultimately, better writers. Others have found that systematic evaluation of students' writing—using the kinds of scoring approaches discussed in the handbook—can be very useful in diagnosing individual students' strengths and weaknesses. And still others use writing tests to select students for placement into advanced or remedial writing courses.

This handbook illustrates the many ways in which writing assessment can be used advantageously in teaching basic writing skills. It also provides specific guidelines for relating writing assessment to day-to-day instruction and for involving students in the writing sample scoring process in order to teach writing skills.

The handbook, moreover, represents a unique treatment of assessment issues—one tailored specifically for the classroom teacher who has no formal background in testing.

Spandel, V., and Stiggins, R. J. *Writing Assessment in the Classroom.* **White Plains, N.Y.: Longman, in press**

This new book for teachers, due for publication in 1988, integrates systematic writing assessment into writing instruction in a way that promotes the development of thinking skills in the writing context. It teaches teachers to evaluate writing samples analytically and to use diagnostic results to plan and carry out effective writing instruction for all students.

Stiggins, R.J. *Evaluating Students by Classroom Observation: Watching Students Grow.* **Washington, D.C.: National Education Association, 1986.**

This publication offers teachers specific, practical guidelines for using performance assessment to measure student behavior and/or products, and specifies procedures to ensure test quality. Stiggins contends that systematic test design and careful quality control make performance assessment an objective, useful, and valuable form of classroom assessment.

To develop quality performance assessments, the author recommends a four-step sequence of specific planning decisions and testing alternatives. Step one involves describing the assessment situation, determining the specific reason for testing, identifying who wants and reads test results, and describing the skills and/or knowledge to be demonstrated. Steps two and three call for a specification of the test activity and task(s) students will be asked to perform and a description of the students' responses to be evaluated. In doing so, the teacher decides (1) whether a process (behavior, procedure) or product (result of doing) is to be rated, (2) what criteria will be used to judge performance, and (3) whether or not students are to be informed of the performance evaluation. Step four requires that the teacher plan rating procedures by selecting scoring methods and evaluators (teacher, another expert, students, or self) and by determining whether students' results will be compared to one another or to a preset standard.

After outlining these essential planning steps, Stiggins specifies key considerations in ensuring quality assessment. These include establishing clear testing purposes, communicating effectively about assessment, maximizing objectivity, and selecting appropriate and economical options, whether one uses preplanned tests of performance or spontaneous observations of classroom behavior. This succinct booklet provides thorough guidance in using observation to measure student performance.

Appendix B

Answers to Quiz
(Pages 20-21)

1. Analysis.   The key word is *functions*.

2. Inference.   The key is *what . . . if*.

3. Recall.   The key word is *define*.

4. Evaluation.   The keys are *which is best* and *why*.

5. Comparison.

6. Evaluation.   The key is that there is a choice to be made and then a justification to be given.

7. Recall.

8. Inference.   The key words are *if* and *what*.

9. Inference.   Generalizations must be drawn on the basis of comparison.

10. Analysis.   The key word is *purposes*.

11. Analysis.   The key word is *functions*.

12. Evaluation.   The key is that a choice must be made and justified.

13. Inference.   The key words are *if*, *which*, and *would*.

14. Analysis.   The key word is *purposes*.

15. Evaluation.   The key is that a choice must be made and a justification given.

16. Analysis.   The key words are *what are some* and *might perform*.

17. Recall.

18. Comparison.   The key is that one particular thing is being compared in three paintings.

19. Inference.   The key words are *suppose* and *how else*.

20. Evaluation.   The keys are the words *which is better* and the necessity for justification.

Appendix C

Cognitive Domain Levels
According to Bloom

If you want to measure:	Use these key words in the exercise:		Examples
Knowledge	list describe define label repeat name	fill in identify what when who	List the parts of speech.
Comprehension	paraphrase explain review match discuss	translate interpret how why	Explain what purpose the verb serves in a sentence.
Application	apply construct draw simulate sketch	employ restructure predict how	Write a sentence that includes a noun, a verb, and a direct object.
Analysis	classify dissect distinguish differentiate compare	contrast categorize separate break down subdivide	Break down this sentence into its component parts by diagramming it.
Synthesis	combine relate put together	integrate assemble collect	Combine what you know about good sentences and good paragraphs to write an essay on. . . .
Evaluation	judge argue assess appraise decide defend	rate debate evaluate choose should	Evaluate this paragraph. Is it good? Why or why not?